Kol Dodi
the voice of my beloved
Jewish Music for Wedding

Music Editor
Mary Feinsinger

Editor-in-Chief, Transcontinental Music Publications
J. Mark Dunn

Kol Dodi Committee
Mary Feinsinger
Cantor Helene Reps
Joyce Rosenzweig
Cantor Benjie-Ellen Schiller
Dr. Judith Tischler

Transcontinental Music Publications

993107

Hebrew Pronunciation Guide

VOWELS
a as in f*a*ther
ai as in *ai*sle (= long *i* as in *i*ce)
e = short *e* as in b*e*d
ei as in *ei*ght (= long *a* as in *a*ce)
i as in p*i*zza (= long *e* as in b*e*)
o = long *o* as in g*o*
u = long *u* as in l*u*nar
' = unstressed vowel close to ə or unstressed short *e*

CONSONANTS
ch as in German Ba*ch* or Scottish lo*ch* (not as in *ch*eese)
g = hard *g* as in **g**et (not soft *g* as in **g**em)
tz = as in boa*ts*
h after a vowel is silent

Yiddish Pronunciation Guide

VOWELS
a as in f*a*ther
ai as in *ai*sle (= long *i* as in *i*ce)
e = short *e* as in b*e*d
ei as in *ei*ght (= long *a* as in *a*ce)
i as in p*i*zza (= long *e* as in b*e*)
o = long *o* as in g*o*
' = unstressed vowel close to ə or unstressed short *e*
u (between consonants) = *u* as in p*u*t
u (at end of word) = long *u* as in l*u*nar

CONSONANTS
ch as in German Ba*ch* or Scottish lo*ch* (not as in *ch*eese)
g = hard *g* as in **g**et (not soft *g* as in **g**em)
tz = as in boa*ts*

Ladino (Judeo-Spanish) Pronunciation Guide

d = Pronounced like "th", as in *th*is
g = Before e or i, like "dj", as in **g**entle
j = Not gutturalized, as in vi*s*ion
ll = Pronounced as "y", as in **y**et
s = When initial - unvoiced, as in *s*orry
When between vowels, - voiced, as in la*z*y
When final - voiced, as in la*z*y
c = Pronounced like unvoiced s, as in *s*orry
z = Voiced s sound, as in la*z*y
x = Pronounced like "sh", as in *sh*oe
v = As "v" in English, as in **v**ictory

To further the planning of your wedding, read the CCAR Press's
Beyond Breaking the Glass: A Spiritual Guide to Your Jewish Wedding by Rabbi Nancy H. Wiener
Visit www.CCARnet.org/press to order your copy!

KOL DODI: JEWISH MUSIC FOR WEDDINGS
©2001 Transcontinental Music Publications/New Jewish Music Press
A Division of the Union of American Hebrew Congregations
633 Third Avenue - New York, NY 10017 - fax 212.650.4109
212.650.4101 - www.eTranscon.com - tmp@uahc.org

Printed in the United States of America
Design by Joel N. Eglash
ISBN 8074-0810-7
10 9 8 7 6 5 4 3 2 1
Ketubah cover art courtesy of The Israel Museum

The Wedding Service ———————

Kol Dodi
the voice of my beloved

Additional Solo Pieces ———————

Folk Service

Baruch Haba/Mi Adir

Danny Maseng

Birkat Erusin

Danny Maseng

Sheva B'rachot

Danny Maseng

Y'varech'cha

Danny Maseng

Sephardic Service

B'ruchim Haba'im

Carpentras tradition, Cremeieu Collection 1885
arranged by Mary Feinsinger

B'ru - chim ha - ba -

im b' - sheim A - do - nai,_____ bei - rach - nu - chem mi - beit_____ A - do - nai.

Bo - u nish - ta - cha - veh v' - nich - ra - ah,_____ niv - r' - cha lif - nei A - do - nai_____ o -

reich et he cha - - - - tan,_____ cha - - - - tan v'et - ha -

ka - - - lah.

Birkat Erusin
(French Sephardic)

from traditional motifs
arranged by Mary Feinsinger

Ba - ruch a - tah Ado - nai E - lo - hei - nu

me - lech ha - o - lam bo - rei p' - ri ha -

ga - fen. Ba - ruch a - tah Ado -

Sheva B'rachot

from traditional motifs
arranged by Mary Feinsinger

nai____ E-lo-hei-nu me-lech__ ha-o-lam_____ she-ha-kol ba - ra lich-vo-

do._____ Ba - ruch a - tah A-do - nai_____ E-lo-hei - nu

me-lech__ ha-o-lam_____ yo - tzeir_____ ha-a-dam.____ Ba -

ruch a-tah A-do-nai E-lo - hei-nu me-lech ha-o - lam_____ a-

sher ya-tzar et ha-a-dam b'-tzal - mo, b'-tze-lem d'-mut tav-ni - to v'-hit-kin

lo mi-me-nu bin-yan a-dei— ad._____ Ba - ruch_____ a - tah— A-do-

nai yo-tzeir_____ ha - a - dam._____ Sos ta-sis v'-ta-

geil ha-a-ka-rah___ b'-ki-butz ba-ne-ha l'-to-chah b'-sim - - chah. Ba-

ruch a-tah A-do-nai___ m'-sa-mei-ach___ Tzi-yon___ b'-va-ne-ha. Sa-

Faster

mei-ach t'-sa-mach re-im ha-a-hu-vim k'-sa-mei-cha-cha y'-tzir-cha b'-

rit. **Tempo I**

gan E-den mi ke-dem, mi-ke-___dem. Ba-ruch a-tah A-do-

nai m'-sa-mei-ach___ cha-tan v'-ka-lah.___ Ba-

Allegro

_ u - v'-chu-tzot Y' - ru-sha-la - yim. Kol sa-son, v' - kol sim-chah,

kol cha-tan v' - kol ka-lah, kol mitz-ha-lot cha-ta-nim mei-chu-pa-tam _ u-n'-a-

Tempo I

rim mi-mish-tei n' - gi - - na-tam. Ba-ruch a - tah _ A-do-

nai _ m'-sa-mei-ach cha-tan _ im ha-ka-lah. _

Y'varech'cha

Yemenite melody
arranged by Mary Feinsinger

"May our God and the God of all ages bless you with the three-fold benediction of the Torah :"

Y' - va - - - - re - ch'-cha A-do - nai_____ v' - yish - - m' - re - cha, yish - m' - re - cha.

"The Lord bless you and keep you."

Ya -

"The Lord look kindly upon
you and be gracious to you."

seim l'-cha sha - lom,_____ sha - lom._____

"May God reach out to you in tenderness, and give you peace."

A - - - - mein.

Classical Service

Commissioned by Cantor R. Bloch

B'ruchim Haba-im

Ben Steinberg

* Tempi are approximate.
Let the piece "flow", throughout

mi ga-dol al ha - kol y' - va -

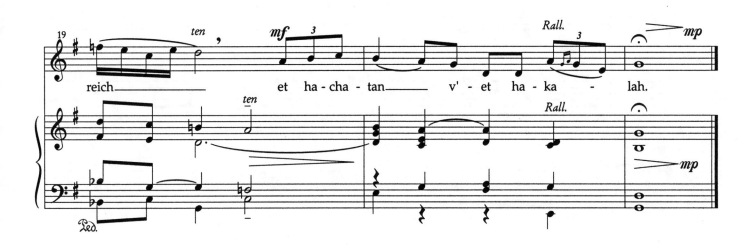

reich et ha-cha - tan v' - et ha - ka - lah.

Birkat Eirusin

Ben Steinberg

hei - nu me-lech ha-o-lam a-sher kid'-sha-nu b'-mitz-vo-tav. V' - tzi -

va - nu al ha-a-ra-yot. V' - a-sar la-nu et ha-a-ru -

sot v'-hi-tir la-nu et han'-su-ot la-nu al y' -

Commissioned by Cantor R. Bloch

Sheva B'rachot

Ben Steinberg

Ba - ruch a - tah A - do - nai E - lo - hei - nu me-lech ha - o-lam bo - rei p' - ri ha - ga - fen.

Ba - ruch a-tah A-do-nai E-lo - hei-nu me-lech ha-o-lam she-ha - kol ba-ra lich-vo-do

Ba - ruch a-tah A-do-nai E-lo - hei - nu me-lech ha-o-lam yo -

Y'varech'cha

Max Helfman

Accompanied Cantorial Service

Baruch Habah

based on *Shir Hashirim cantillation*

Lawrence Avery

Birkat Erusin

Ario S. Hyams
arr. Mary Feinsinger

Ba - ruch a - tah A - do - nai   E - lo - hei - nu me - lech ha - o - lam____

bo - rei p' - ri____ ha - ga - fen.   Ba - ruch a - tah A - do - nai   E - lo - hei - nu me - lech ha - o -

lam____ a - sher kid' - sha - nu b' - mitz - vo - tav   v' - hi - tir la - nu____ al y' - dei chu - pah v' - ki - du - shin. Ba -

ruch a - tah A - do - nai,   m' - ka - deish a - mo Yis - ra - eil al y' - dei chu - pah____ v' - ki - du - shin.

Sheva B'rachot

Traditional
arr. Morris Barash

48

kol mitz-ha-lot cha-ta-nim mei-chu-pa-tam u-n'-a-rim mi-mish-teih n'-gi-na-tam____

Ba - ruch_____ a - tah A - do - nai ____ m'-sa-

mei - ach m'-sa-mei-ach cha-tan____ im____ ha ka - lah.____

Y'varech'cha

Max Janowski

Y'-va-re-ch'cha A-do-nai____ v'-yish-m're-cha v'-

yish-m're-cha Ya-eir____ A-do-nai____ pa-nav____ ei-

le-cha vi-chu-ne-ka Yi-sa____ Yi-

Originally scored for Cantor, Choir, and Organ

Unaccompanied Cantorial Service

B'ruchim Haba-im

Alberto Mizrahi

arranged by Mary Feinsinger

58

Birkat Erusin

Alberto Mizrahi
arranged by Mary Feinsinger

Sheva B'rachot

Alberto Mizrahi
arranged by Mary Feinsinger

hei - nu me - lech___ ha - o

tzeir_____ ha -

hei - nu me - lech ha - o - lam___ yo - tzeir_____ ha -

a - - - dam.

a - - - dam. 4. Ba - ruch a - tah A-do - nai___ E-lo - hei-nu me - lech__ ha-o -

lam a - sher ya - tzar et ha - a-dam b' - tzal - mo_____ b' -

v' - hit - kin lo_____ mi - mei - nu bin -

tze - lem d' - mut___ tav - ni - to v' - hit-kin lo_____ mi-mei - nu bin -

yan a - dei ad.

tzer_____

yan a - dei ad. Ba - ruch a - tah A-do - nai yo - tzer_____

64

Y'varech'cha

Alberto Mizrahi
arranged by Mary Feinsinger

Additional Solo Pieces

A Yidishe Khasene (Medley)

arranged by Mary Feinsinger

Hey Klezmorim
(Mani Leib, Julius Keil)

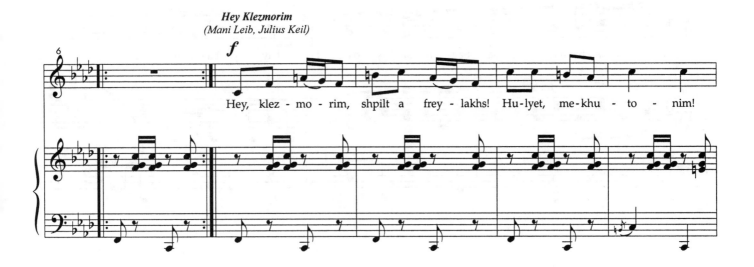

Hey, klez - mo - rim, shpilt a frey - lakhs! Hu - lyet, me - khu - to - nim!

Trinkt un zayt zikh mes - sa - mey - akh, oyf - tse - pu - ke - nish di so - nim. Trinkt un zayt zikh

mes - sa - mey - akh, oyf - tse - pu - ke - nish di so - nim! Ay,

ya - ba - ba - ba - bay, ba - ba - bay, ba - ba - bay - bay. Hay - bay ya - ba - ba - ba - bay.

Hay! Ya - ba - ba - ba - bay, ba - ba - bay, ba - ba - bay - bay. Bay - bay bi - di - bi - di

Di Mekhutonim Geyen
(M. M. Warshawsky)

bam!   Di   me-khu-

to-nim gey-en, kin - der Lo-mir zikh frey-en— shat nor, shat! Der kho-sn iz gor a

vin - der Shpilt a vi-vat dem kho-sns tsad, Yay-bay!   Yay-bay!

72

Hay bay ti - di - bi - di - bam. Yay - bay! Yay - bay! Ay - ay - ay - ay

ay - yay - yay.

poco rit.

Meno Mosso

In Rod Arayn
(L. Kogan)

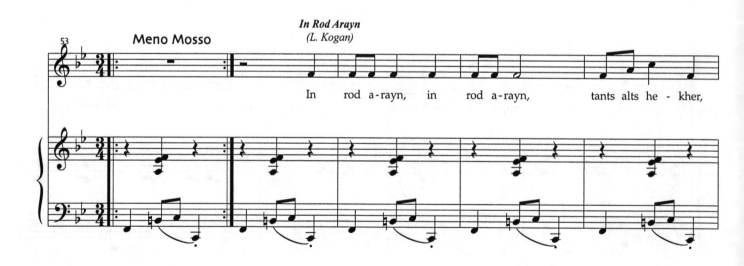

In rod a - rayn, in rod a - rayn, tants alts he - kher,

he - kher. S'iz ba undz di sim-khe groys, to gist on ful dem be - kher.

Tants, tants, tants a bi - se - le mit mir. Ikh hob lib di

ey - dems un du host lib di shnir. Tants, tants, tants a

bi - se - le mit mir. Ikh hob lib di ey - dems un du host lib di

Allegro

shnir.

Mekhuteneste Mayne
folk, M. Beregovsek, I. Feffer

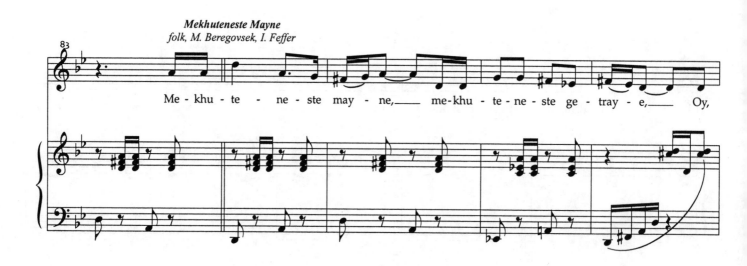

Me - khu - te - ne - ste may - ne,___ me - khu - te - ne - ste ge - tray - e,___ Oy,

lo - mir zayn oyf ey - bik me-khu-to - - - nim. Oy, lo - mir zayn oyf ey - bik me-khu -

to - - - nim. Ikh gib___ aykh a - vek mayn tokh-ter far a shnir Zi

zol bay aykh nit on - ve - rn dos po - - - nim. Ikh gib___ aykh a - vek mayn

tokh-ter far a shnir Zi zol bay aykh nit on-ve-rn dos po — — nim.

Tantst, tantst, me-ku - te - ne - ste,_____ tantst a mits-ve ten - tsl.

Di Mezinke Oysgegebn
M. M. Warshawsky

He - kher, be - ser___ Di rod, di rod makht

gre-ser. Groys hot mikh got ge-makht Glik hot er mir ge-brakht.

Hu-lyet, kin-der, a gan-tse nakht. Di mi-zin-ke oys-ge-

ge-bn,__ Di mi-zin-ke oys-ge-ge-bn,__ Di mi-zin-ke oys-ge-ge-bn,__ Di mi-zin-ke oys-ge-

Molto Allegro

Khosn Kale Mazl Tov
traditional

ge - bn. Ay - yay - yay kho - sn ka - le ma - zl tov!____ Ay - yay - yay

kho - sn ka - le ma - zl tov!____ Ay - yay - yay kho - sn ka - le

ma - zl tov!____Ay - yay - yay yay yay Yay - yay - yay - yay Yay! Ay - yay - yay kho - sn ka - le

An Invitation

Songs of Wine
Sh'muel HaNagid

Rachelle Nelson

My love tell me when shall I pour— you— my—

1.
wine,_____ — my

2.

fore_ the dawn starts to rise,_____ to rise,_____ the

nec - tar of spiced po - ma - gran - ate_____

_____ From the per - fumed hand of_____ a_

1985

Anah Dodi

Song of Songs 2: 10-13

Max Janowski

A-nah do-di—— v'-a-mar——li

Ku-mi lach ra-ya-ti ya-fa-ti u-l'-chi-lach Ki hi-

neih—— ha-s'-tav a-var Ha-ge-shemcha-laf ha-lach lo ha-ge-shem cha-laf ha-

lach lo—— Ha-ni-tza-

Anah Dodi

Song of Songs: 2:10, 11

Rachelle Nelson

Anah Halach Dodeich

Song of Songs 6:1,2

Folk Tune
arranged by Mary Feinsinger

Arise and Come Away

Song of Songs 2: 12, 14; 6:3; 8:6; 4:16

Mary Feinsinger

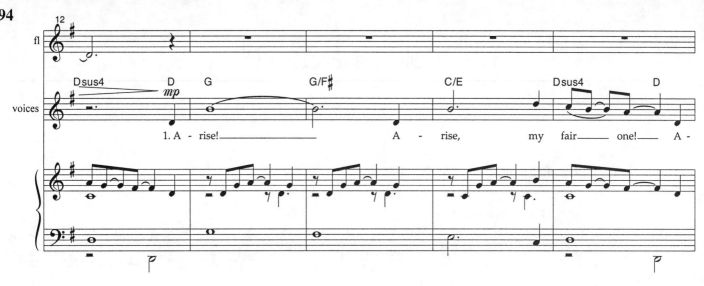

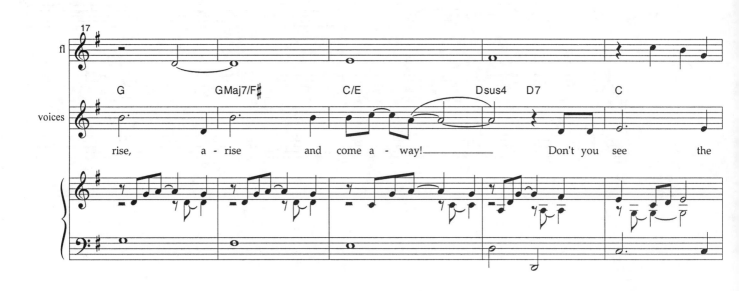

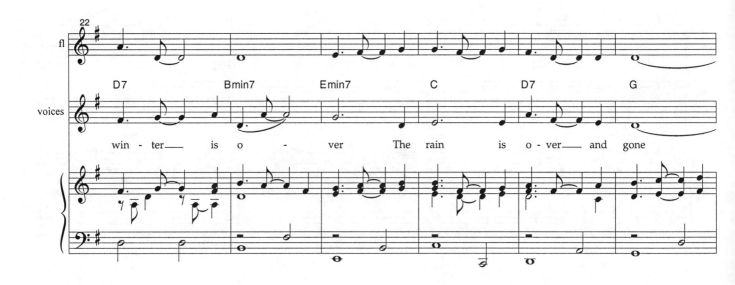

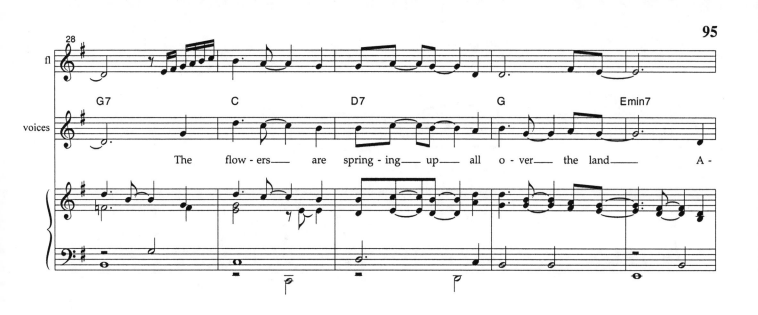

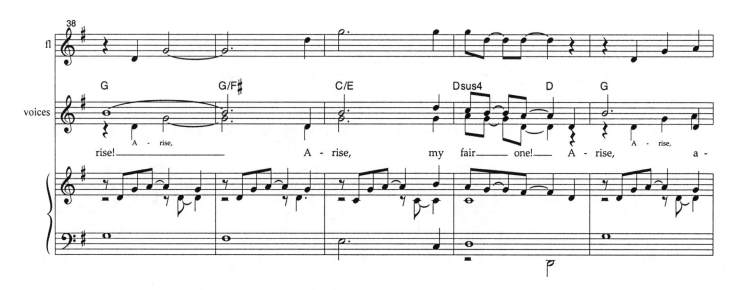

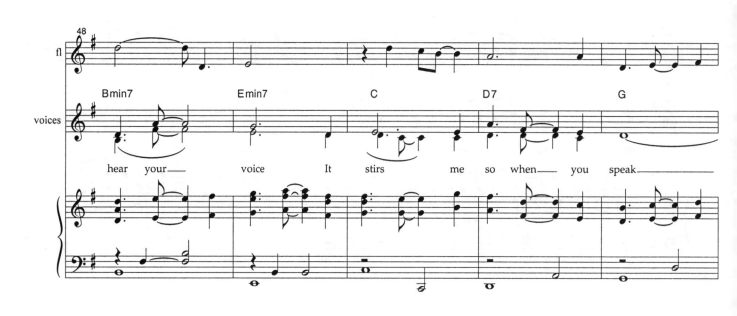

Der Badkhn

Lyrics: Itsik Manger

Henekh Kon
arranged by Mary Feinsinger

1. Kho - sn un ka - le me-khu - to - nim un fraynt_____ nor_____
zitst do di ka - le_____ sheyn vi der tog_____ Un di
zitst do der kho - sn_____ in sa - met un zayd_____ Un_____
trakht nor dem bad - khn_____ vos do far aykh shteyt_____ Un

Hert vos es dar - shnt der bad - khn haynt_____ Di
vos zogt di fi - dl? Zog, fi - de - le, zog_____ Me-khu -
ka - le shaynt in ir khu - pe - kleyd._____ Er
redt tsu aykh klu - ge un tay - e - re reyd._____ Er

["The badkhn was an important and integral part of the [Jewish] wedding celebration, particularly in Poland and the Ukraine...his double task was [that of] evoking laughter from the guests and tears from the bride and groom." Ruth Rubin, *Voices of a People* p. 100ff]

Dodi Li

Song of Songs 2:16, 3:6

Danny Maseng

Do - di li va-a-ni lo ha-ro-
eh ba - sho - sha - nim.
Do - di li va-a-ni lo ha-ro-eh ba - sho - sha -
nim.
Hi - nach ya - fah ra - ya - ti, ra - ya -
ti.
Hi - nach ya - fah ei - na - yich yo - nim. Do -
di li va-a-ni lo ha-ro-eh ba - sho - sha - nim.

Dodi Li

N. Chen
arranged by Mary Feinsinger

Shir HaShirim 2:16, 3:6, 4:9, 16

Dodi Li

Song of Songs 2:16, 3:6, 4:9

Steven Sher
arranged by Mary Feinsinger

vo — — — nah, u – l' – vo — — di — nah. Do – di –

li. Do — di li, va – a –

ni lo ha – ro – eh ba – sho — – sha – nim.

Do — di li, do – di li.

El Ginat Egoz

Sara Levy-Tanai
arranged by Mary Feinsinger

Shir HaShirim 6:11, 7:12, 13

ri - mo - nim.

presto subito

Tempo I

L' - chah do - di nei - tzei ha - sa - deh___ na - li - nah bak' - fa - rim. Nash -

ki - mah lak' - ra - mim nir - eh im - par - chah ha - ge - fen pi - tach___ has' -

ma - dar.

presto subito

Erev Shel Shoshanim

M. Dor

Y. Hadar
arranged by Mary Feinsinger

E - rev shel sho-sha - nim⸺ nei - tzei na el ha - bus - tan.

mor, be - sa - mim u - l' - vo - nah l' - rag' - lech mif' - tan.

Lai - lah yo - reid l' - at_____ v' - ru - ach sho - shan nosh - va

ha - vah el - chash lach shir ba - lat ze - mer shel a - ha - vah.

Sha - char ho - mah yo - nah_____ ro - sheich ma - lei t'la - lim

How Beautiful You Are

Song of Songs 1:16-17

Srul Irving Glick

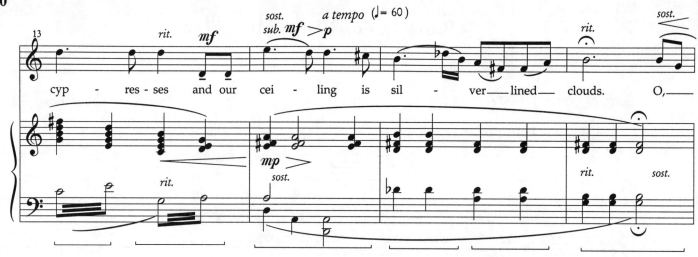

cyp - res - ses   and   our   cei - ling   is   sil - ver   lined   clouds.   O,

how   beau - ti - ful   you   are   my   love   my   love.

(* Original has only "d" and "e".)

For my daughter, Althea

I Am My Beloved's

Song of Songs 6:3, 2:10-13

Maurice Goldman

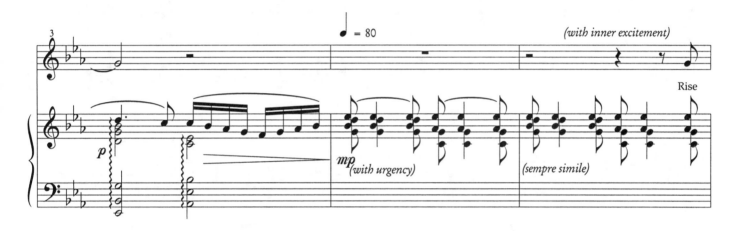

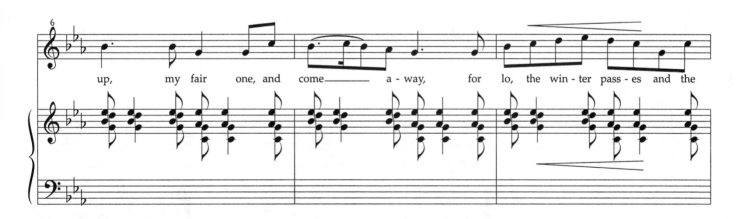

Iti Milvanon

Nira Chen
arranged by Mary Feinsinger

Song of Songs 4:8, 4:1, 5:16

I - ti____ mi - l' - va - non,____ i - ti ka - la ta - vo - - - i Hi - nach ya - fah____ - ra - ya - ti____ ei - na - - - yich yo - nim.____ - Mi - mo - not____ a - ra - yot mei - rosh____ shir

Kumi Lach

Debbie Friedman
arranged by Julie Silver
transcribed for keyboard by Mary Feinsinger

Song of Songs 2: 10

Ku - mi— lach,_____ ku - mi— lach ra - ya - ti ya - fa - ti, kumi—

lach._____ lach._____ Ki - hi - nei has - tav,_____

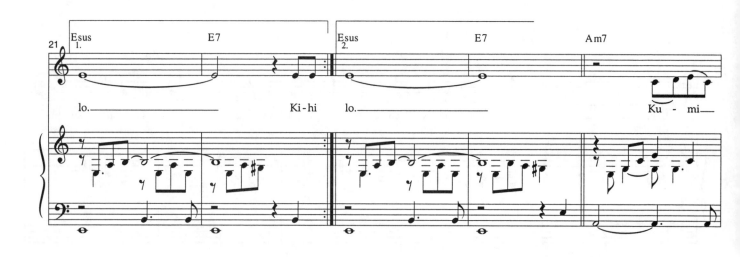

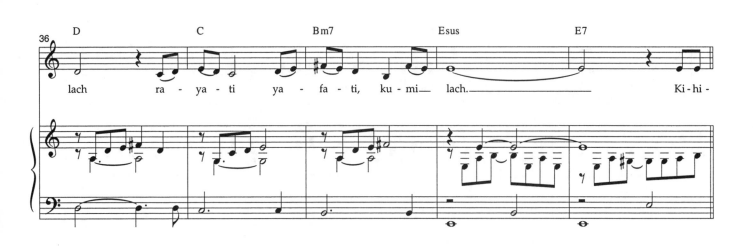

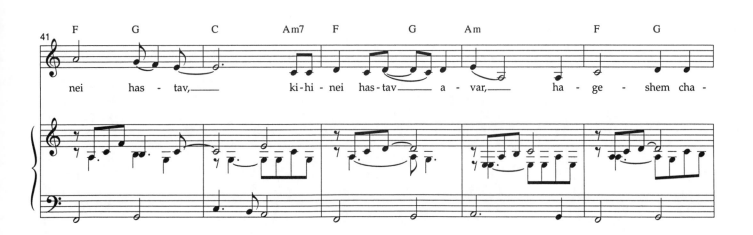

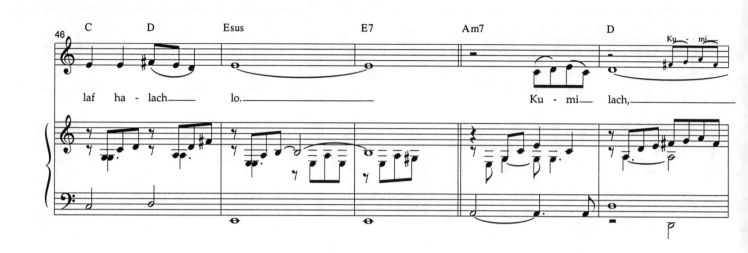

Los Bilbilicos

Sephardic Folk
arranged by Mary Feinsinger

Los bil - bi - li - cos— can - - tan con so-
spi - ros de— a - mor. Los bil - bi - li - cos—
can - tan con so-spi-ros de— a - mor. Mi ne-sha - ma y mi ven-

poco piu moso

tu - - ra es - tan en tu po - der_____ Mi ne-

sha - ma y mi ven-tu_____ ra es - tan en tu po-der_____ 2.Mas

pres - to ven_ pa - lom - - ba,___ mas pres - to ven_ con

mi_____ Mas pres - to ven_ pa - lom - - ba,___ mas

Papir Iz Dokh Vays

Y. L. Cahan

E. Zunser (1836-1913)
arranged by Mary Feinsinger

1. Pa - pir iz dokh vays un tint iz dokh shvarts. Tsu
3. Dayn tal - ye, dayn mi - ne, dayn ey - de - ler fa - son, In

dir, mayn zis le - bn tzit dokh mayn harts. Kh'volt shten - dik ge -
hart - sn brent a fay - er me zet es nit on; Ni - to a za -

ze - sn dray teg nokh a - nand Tzu ku - shn dayn sheyn po - nim, tzu
mentsh vos zol fi - ln vi es brent Der toyt un dos le - bn iz bay

hal - tn dayn hant.
got in di hent.

2. Nekh - tn, ba - nakht bin ikh oyf a kha - se - ne ge - ven. Fil shey - ne
4. Akh, du li - ber Got, her oys mayn far - lang. Dem oy - sher gi - stn

Scalerica De Oro

Ladino
arranged by Richard J. Neumann

Sca-le-ri-ca de o-ro, de o-ro y de mar-
fil Pa-ra que su-va la no-via a dar ki-du-

* The ms. is unclear, but Neumann seems to want a flute, if possible, to play whenever there is a florid upper line in the piano.

shin. Ve - ni - mos a ver,_____ ve - ni - mos a ver Y go - zen y lo - gren y ten - gan mun - cho bien. Ve—

bien.

(last time to ⊕ Coda)

(last time to ⊕ Coda)

1. La_____ no - via no tie - ne di - ne - ro,_____
2. La_____ no - via no tie - ne con - ta - do,_____

La_____ no - via no tie - ne di - ne - ro.
La_____ no - via no tie - ne con - ta - do.

Que_ mos_ ten - ga un ma - zal bue - no!_

al - to! Ve –

Repeat Refrain & Ritornello (D.S. ℅)

Repeat Refrain & Ritornello (D.S. ℅)

CODA

CODA

For the Wedding of Linda and Paul Saiger

Sh'neihem

B'reishit Rabah 8:9, 22:2

Michael Isaacson

Keyboard realization in Seasons in Time, Vol. 1. TMP (991310)

Shir Hashirim

Song of Songs 1:1,2; 3:2; 8:14

based on Vinaver, abridged

Shir ha-shi-rim a-sher lish-lo-mo yi-sha-kei-ni min-shi-kot pi-hu, ki to-vim do-de-cha mi-ya-yin. A-ku-mah na va-a-sov-va va-ir Bash-va-kim u-var-cho-vot a-vak-shah eit she-a-ha-vah naf-shi, bi-kash-tiv v'-lo m'-tza-tiv. B'-rach do-di ud-mei l-cha litz-vi o l'-o-fer ha-a-ya-lim al ha-rei v'-sa-mim.

Shir HaShirim - (Georgian)

Song of Songs 1: 1-4

arranged by Lazar Saminsky

a-la-mot____ a-la-mot a-hei-vu-cha____ Mosh-che-ni a-cha-rei-cha na-ru-tzah

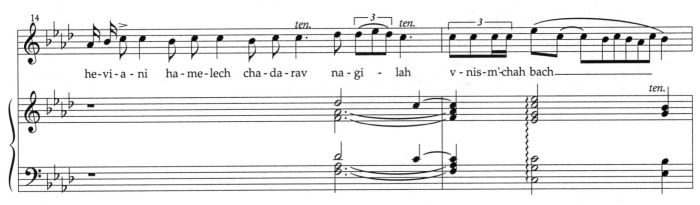

he-vi-a-ni ha-me-lech cha-da-rav na-gi-lah v-nis-m'chah bach____

naz-ki-rah do-de-cha____ mi-ya-yin me-sha-rim____ a-hei-vu-cha____

Simeini Chachotam

Song of Songs 8:6

Charles Davidson

Si - mei-ni cha-cho-tam al li - be - cha, Si-

mei-ni cha-cho-tam al li - be - cha, Si - mei - ni cha-cho-tam

al li-be - cha, cha-cho-tam— al z'-ro-e-cha. Ki a-zah— cha-

Solo or Sops.

al li-be - cha, Si - mei-ni cha-cho-tam al li-be - cha cha-cho-tam

al z'-ro - e-cha, cha-cho-tam al z'-ro-e-cha.

poco rit.

Dedicated to Ken and Jennifer Litwin

V'eirastich Li

Hosea 2:21-22

Bonia Shur
ASCAP

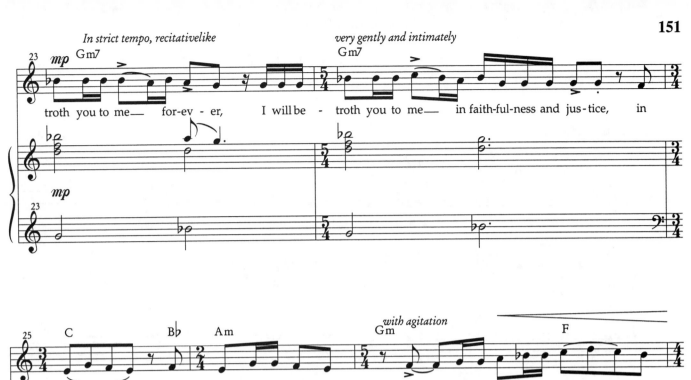

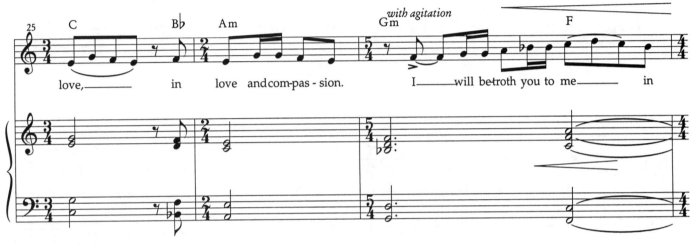

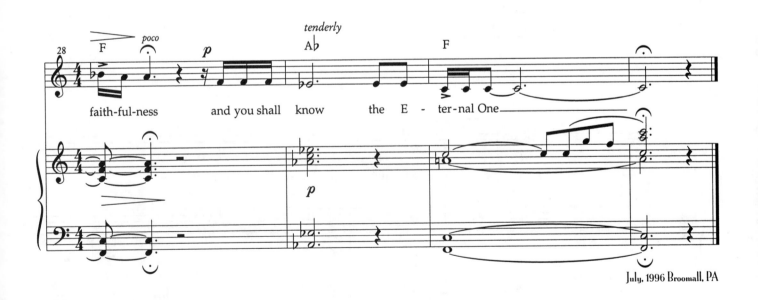

July, 1996 Broomall, PA

In honor of Dr. Bernard Shapiro

V'eirastich Li

Hosea 2:21-22

Ben Steinberg

Yismach Chatan

Joseph Blumberg

Leon Algazi

You Have Captured My Heart

Based on Song of Songs

music and lyrics by Julie Silver
piano arrangement by Mary Feinsinger

When the wind blows____ gent - ly

and the shad - ows flee_____ I will take you to the

So look to me my___ dar - - - ling,___

For the Wedding of William and Denice Bronstein

Song of Songs 5:16
United Synagogue K'tubah, adapted by Lester Bronstein

Benji Ellen Schiller

Zeh do - di, zeh re - i, This is my be - lov - ed.

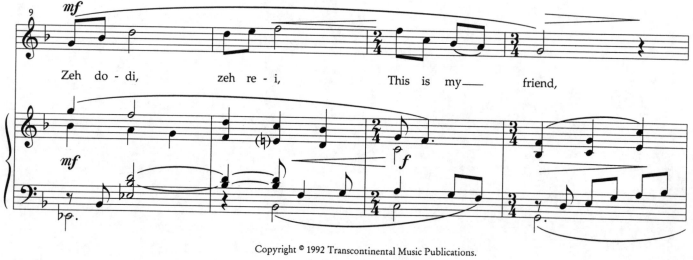

Zeh do - di, zeh re - i, This is my friend,

TRANSLATIONS

Anah Dodi – Shir haShirim 2:10-13

עָנָה דוֹדִי וְאָמַר לִי קוּמִי לָךְ רַעְיָתִי יָפָתִי וּלְכִי-לָךְ׃ כִּי-הִנֵּה הַסְּתָו עָבָר הַגֶּשֶׁם חָלַף הָלַךְ לוֹ׃ הַנִּצָּנִים נִרְאוּ בָאָרֶץ עֵת הַזָּמִיר הִגִּיעַ וְקוֹל הַתּוֹר נִשְׁמַע בְּאַרְצֵנוּ׃ הַתְּאֵנָה חָנְטָה פַגֶּיהָ וְהַגְּפָנִים סְמָדַר נָתְנוּ רֵיחַ קוּמִי לָךְ רַעְיָתִי יָפָתִי וּלְכִי-לָךְ׃

Thus my beloved spoke to me:
Arise my darling, my fair one, come away!
For lo the winter is past,
the rain is over and gone
The blossoms have appeared in the land
the pruning time has come;
The song of the turtledove is heard in our land.
The green figs form on the fig tree,
The vines in blossom give off fragrance.
Arise my darling,
my fair one, come away!

Anah Halach Dodeich – Shir haShirim 6:1-2

אָנָה הָלַךְ דּוֹדֵךְ הַיָּפָה בַּנָּשִׁים אָנָה פָּנָה דוֹדֵךְ וּנְבַקְשֶׁנּוּ עִמָּךְ׃ דּוֹדִי יָרַד לְגַנּוֹ לַעֲרֻגוֹת הַבֹּשֶׂם׃

"Where has your loved one gone,
O fairest from among the women?
Where has your beloved turned?
Let us look for him with you."
My love has gone down to his garden,
to the beds of spices,
to browse in the gardens and to pick the lilies.

Dodi Li – Shir haShirim 2:16, 3:6, 4:9, 16

דּוֹדִי לִי וַאֲנִי לוֹ הָרֹעֶה בַּשּׁוֹשַׁנִּים׃
י זֹאת עֹלָה מִן-הַמִּדְבָּר מְקֻטֶּרֶת מוֹר וּלְבוֹנָה
לִבַּבְתִּנִי אֲחֹתִי כַלָּה לִבַּבְתִּינִי׃
עוּרִי צָפוֹן וּבוֹאִי תֵימָן׃

My beloved is mine and I am his.
Who browses among the lilies
Who is she that comes up from the desert
In clouds of myrrh and frankincense
You have captured my heart,
my own, my bride,
you have captured my heart.
Awake, O North wind,
Come, O South wind!

El Ginat Egoz - Shir haShirim 6:11, 7:12, 13

אֶל-גִּנַּת אֱגוֹז יָרַדְתִּי לִרְאוֹת בְּאִבֵּי הַנָּחַל לִרְאוֹת הֲפָרְחָה הַגֶּפֶן הֵנֵצוּ הָרִמֹּנִים׃
לְכָה דוֹדִי נֵצֵא הַשָּׂדֶה נָלִינָה בַּכְּפָרִים׃
נַשְׁכִּימָה לַכְּרָמִים נִרְאֶה אִם פָּרְחָה הַגֶּפֶן פִּתַּח הַסְּמָדַר׃

I went down to the nut grove
To see the budding of the vale;
To see if the vines had blossomed,
If the pomegranates were in bloom.
Come, my love,
Let us go into the open;
Let us lodge among the henna shrubs.
Let us go to the vineyards early;
Let us see if the vine has flowered,

Erev Shel Shoshanim

עֶרֶב שֶׁל שׁוֹשַׁנִּים נֵצֵא נָא אֶל הַבֻּסְתָּן מוֹר בְּשָׂמִים וּלְבוֹנָה לְרַגְלֵךְ מִפְתָּן. לַיְלָה יוֹרֵד
לְאַט וְרוּחַ שׁוֹשָׁן נוֹשְׁבָה הָבָה אֶלְחַשׁ לָךְ שִׁיר בַּלָּאט, זֶמֶר שֶׁל אַהֲבָה. שַׁחַר הוֹמָה
יוֹנָה רֹאשֵׁךְ מָלֵא טְלָלִים פִּיךְ אֶל הַבֹּקֶר שׁוֹשַׁנָּה אֶקְטְפֶנּוּ לִי.

An evening fragrant with roses;
let us go out to the orchard.
Myrrh, spices and frankincense shall be as a
threshold for your feet.

Iti Milvanon - Shir haShirim 4:8, 4:1, 5:16

אִתִּי מִלְּבָנוֹן אִתִּי כַּלָּה תָּבוֹאִי
הִנָּךְ יָפָה רַעְיָתִי עֵינַיִךְ יוֹנִים
מִמְּעֹנוֹת אֲרָיוֹת מֵרֹאשׁ שְׂנִיר וְחֶרְמוֹן
זֶה דוֹדִי וְזֶה רֵעִי בְּנוֹת יְרוּשָׁלָ͏ִם זֶה דוֹדִי

With me from Lebanon
With me, my bride – come!
You are fair my darling,
Ah, You are fair.
Your eyes are like doves.
From the dens of lions,
From the Senir and Hermon
Such is my beloved,
such is my darling,
O maidens of Jerusalem.

Simeini Chachotam – Shir haShirim 8:6

שִׂימֵנִי כַחוֹתָם עַל-לִבֶּךָ כַּחוֹתָם עַל-זְרוֹעֶךָ כִּי-עַזָּה כַמָּוֶת אַהֲבָה קָשָׁה כִשְׁאוֹל
קִנְאָה רְשָׁפֶיהָ רִשְׁפֵּי אֵשׁ שַׁלְהֶבֶתְיָה׃

Let me be a seal upon your heart,
like the seal upon your hand.
For love is fierce as death,
Passion is strong as Sheol;
Its darts are darts of fire,
a blazing flame.

וְאֵרַשְׂתִּיךְ לִי לְעוֹלָם וְאֵרַשְׂתִּיךְ לִי בְּצֶדֶק וּבְמִשְׁפָּט וּבְחֶסֶד וּבְרַחֲמִים
וְאֵרַשְׂתִּיךְ לִי בֶּאֱמוּנָה וְיָדַעַתְּ אֶת־יְהֹוָה׃

And I will espouse you forever:
I will espouse you with righteousness and justice,
and with goodness and mercy,
And I will betroth you to me with faithfulness;
Then you shall be devoted to the Eternal One.

Baruch Haba (B'ruchim Haba-im)

May the one who enters be blessed in the name of Adonai; we bless you from the House of Adonai.
Adonai is God; God has given us light; bind the festal offering to the horns of the altar with cords.
You are my God and I will praise You; You are my God, I will extol You. Praise Adonai for God is good; God's steadfast love is eternal.

Birkat Erusin

We praise You, Eternal God, Sovereign of the universe, Creator of the fruit of the vine.
We praise You, Eternal God, Sovereign of the universe, who hallows us with Mitzvot and consecrates this marriage.
We praise You, Eternal God, who sanctifies our people Israel through *Kiddushin*, the sacred rite of marriage at the *Chuppah*.

Sheva Brachot

1. We praise You, Eternal God, Sovereign of the universe, Creator of the fruit of the vine.
2. We praise You, Eternal God, Sovereign of the universe, Creator of all things for Your glory.
3. We praise You, Eternal God, Sovereign of the universe, Creator of man and woman.
4. We praise You, Eternal God, Sovereign of the universe, Creator of man and woman, who has fashioned us in Your image and has established marriage for the fulfillment and perpetuation of life in accordance with Your holy purpose. We praise You, Eternal God, Creator of man and woman.
5. You have filled Zion's mouth with song: her children have come back to her in joy! We give thanks to the One who gladdens Zion through her children.
6. We praise You, Eternal God, who causes bride and groom to rejoice. May these loving companions rejoice as have Your creatures since the days of creation.
7. We praise You, Eternal God, Sovereign of the universe, Creator of joy and gladness, bride and groom, love and kinship, peace and friendship. O God, may there always be heard in the cities of Israel and in the streets of Jerusalem: the sounds of joy and of happiness, the voice of the groom and the voice of the bride, the shouts of young people celebrating, and the songs of children at play. We praise You, Eternal God, who causes the bride and groom to rejoice together.

Y'varech'cha

May God bless you and keep you.
May God look kindly upon you, and be gracious to you.
May God reach out to you in tenderness, and give you peace.

YIDDISH

A Yidishe Khasene
Hey Klezmorim
Hey musicians, play a joyful tune! Drink and be joyful in spite of your enemies.

Di Mekhutonim Geyen
The in-laws are coming, children, let us rejoice – quiet, quiet! The groom is quite a wonder, hooray for the groom's side.

In Rod Arayn
Join the circle, dance livelier! Our celebration is great, so fill up the goblet! Dance, dance, dance a little with me! You're partial to the groom and I'm partial to the bride.

Mekhuteneste Mayne
Dearest Mekhuteneste (mother of child's spouse), let's always be good inlaws. I'm giving you my daughter as a daughter-in-law. May she not lose her looks with you!

Di Mizinke Oysgegebn
Louder, livelier, make the dance-ring wider! God has brought me good fortune. My youngest daughter is getting married, so rejoice with me.

Khosn Kale Mazl Tov
Groom and bride, congratulations!

Der Badkhn
Bridegroom and bride, family and friends – hear what the badkhn (wedding jester) has to say:
"On this happy and joyous day, the violin trembles and the flute sobs: 'Beauty is lovely, but beauty doesn't last. Life and good fortune are but shadows, which vanish as a shadow vanishes, never to return.'"

Thus speaks the badkhn, with a tear in his eye.

The bridegroom and bride, family and honored guests are decked in their wedding finery. Yet over all the violin trembles and the flute sobs. Ponder the badkhn's wise and caring words: "Ay, one day the badkhn too will be gone."

Papir Iz Dokh Vays

As surely as paper is white and ink is black, so does my heart yearn for you. I could sit for three whole days, kissing your sweet face and holding your hand.

Last night I went to a wedding, where I saw many pretty girls there; but none could compare with you, with your lovely black eyes and raven hair.

Your figure, your face, your gentle ways, have kindled a flame in my heart, but no one can see it burning. Dear God, all I want is a little house in a meadow where my sweet love and I can live together.

LADINO

Los Bilbilicos
The nightingale sings with sighs of love. My soul and my fate are in your hands.
The rose blooms in the month of May. My soul and my fate suffer from love's pain.
Come more quickly, dove, more quickly come with me. More quickly come, beloved, run and save me.

Scalerica de Oro
A ladder of gold and ivory so our little bride can go up and take her marriage vows.
We've come to see, we've come to see, may they have joy and prosper and always be happy.
The bride has no money, may they have good fortune. The bride has no riches, may they have good luck.

OTHER JEWISH MUSIC
APPROPRIATE FOR WEDDINGS

from Ruth

Al Tifg'i Vi	Lawrence Avery	Composer
Al Tifg'i Vi	Ben Steinberg	Composer
Al Tifg'i Vi	Simon Sargon	Transcontinental Music
Aria of Ruth	M. Castelnuovo-Tedesco	Mills Music
Don't Ask Me to Leave You	Aminadav Aloni	Composer
Entreat Me Not to Leave Thee	Maurice Goldman	Transcontinental Music
Entreat Me Not to Leave Thee	Max Janowski	Transcontinental Music
Ruth and Naomi	J. Klepper & D. Freelander	Tara Publications
Ruth and Naomi	Linda Hirschhorn	Tara Publications
Song of Ruth	Charles Feldman	Composer
Song of Ruth	Kurt Weill	Chappell & Co.

Service Music

A Jewish Wedding Ceremony	Gershon Kingsley	Transcontinental Music
A Wedding Celebration	Aminadav Aloni	Transcontinental Music
Barash Collection (*Sheva B'rachot*)	Morris Barash	Sacred Music Press
Cantorial Anthology, Vol. V	Gershon Ephros	Transcontinental Music
Cantor's Manual (ACC)		American Conference of Cantors
Cantor's Manual (CA)		Cantors Assembly
Kol Sason (rental)	Michael Isaacson	Transcontinental Music
Kol Simchah (rental)	Michael Isaacson	Transcontinental Music
Marriage Service	Moshe Ganchoff, ed. Schall	Cantors Assembly
Music for a Jewish-American Wedding	Randolph Lowell Dreyfuss	Transcontinental Music
Sheva B'rachot	Aminadav Aloni	Transcontinental Music

Shir haShirim (Song of Songs)

Come, My Beloved	Jack Gottlieb	Theophilus Music
How Fine You Are	C. Colby Sachs	Transcontinental Music
I Am the Rose	Catherine Aks	Transcontinental Music
My Sister, My Bride	C. Colby Sachs	Transcontinental Music
Rise Up My Love	Gershon Kingsley	Transcontinental Music
Seal My Heart	M. Castelnuovo-Tedesco	Transcontinental Music
Set Me As a Seal	Max Helfman	Transcontinental Music
Shir HaShirim	William Sharlin	Transcontinental Music
The Voice of My Beloved	Max Helfman	Transcontinental Music

Other Solo Pieces

Ani Chinor L'shirayich	Michael Isaacson	Transcontinental Music
I Will Betroth You	Simon Sargon	Transcontinental Music
One Song Ago	Aminadav Aloni	Composer
Song for a Marriage	Ben Steinberg	Transcontinental Music
Tavas L'vavi	Aminadav Aloni	Composer
V'eirastich Li	Max Janowski	Transcontinental Music
V'eirastich Li	M. Castelnuovo-Tedesco	Transcontinental Music
V'eirastich Li	Aminadav Aloni	Composer

Instrumental Music

A Wedding Celebration	Aminadav Aloni	Transcontinental Music
Hey Klezmorim!: Instrumental Music for Weddings (Vol. II of *Kol Dodi: Jewish Music for Weddings*)		
	ed. J. Mark Dunn	Transcontinental Music
Jewish Folksongs for String Quartet	arr. Matt Springer	Tara Publications
Klezmer Wedding Band Folio	ed. Velvel Pasternak	Tara Publications
Song of Songs String Quartet #2	Herbert Fromm	Transcontinental Music
The Joy of the Jewish Wedding	ed. Velvel Pasternak	Tara Publications
Wedding Suite	Sidney Friedman	Transcontinental Music